The Life Cycle Series

The Life Cycle of an

ANT

Hadley Dyer & Bobbie Kalman

Crabtree Publishing Company

www.crabtreebooks.com

The Life Cycle Series

A Bobbie Kalman Book

Dedicated by Crystal Foxton
To Ray and Marion Foxton, for being such caring and loving grandparents

Editor-in-Chief
Bobbie Kalman

Writing team
Hadley Dyer
Bobbie Kalman

Substantive editor
Kathryn Smithyman

Project editor
Reagan Miller

Editors
Molly Aloian
Kelley MacAulay

Design
Margaret Amy Salter
Samantha Crabtree (cover)

Production coordinator
Heather Fitzpatrick

Photo research
Crystal Foxton

Consultant
Patricia Loesche, Ph.D., Animal Behavior Program,
Department of Psychology, University of Washington

Illustrations
Katherine Kantor: pages 11 (background), 22, 28, 29, 31 (soil)
Bonna Rouse: back cover, pages 5, 6, 10, 11 (all except background),
   17, 19, 26
Margaret Amy Salter: pages 7, 27, 31 (all except soil)

Photographs
Densey Clyne/ANTPhoto.com: page 17
BigStockPhoto.com: Steve Ellis: page 28; Lyle Koehnlein: page 14
© Scott Camazine: page 18
iStockphoto.com/Jeridu: pages 8, 10, 21 (top)
© Dwight Kuhn: page 12
Alex Wild, www.myrmecos.net: pages 6, 9 (bottom), 13, 15, 16, 19,
   20, 21 (bottom), 24, 25, 26, 27
Other images by Brand X Pictures, Digital Vision, and
   Otto Rogge Photography

Crabtree Publishing Company

www.crabtreebooks.com   1-800-387-7650

Cataloging-in-Publication Data
Dyer, Hadley.
   The life cycle of an ant / Hadley Dyer & Bobbie Kalman.
      p. cm. -- (The life cycle series)
   Includes index.
   ISBN-13: 978-0-7787-0670-0 (rlb)
   ISBN-10: 0-7787-0670-2 (rlb)
   ISBN-13: 978-0-7787-0700-4 (pbk)
   ISBN-10: 0-7787-0700-8 (pbk)
   1. Ants--Life cycles--Juvenile literature. I. Kalman, Bobbie. II. Title.
   QL568.F7D94 2005
   595.79'6--dc22
                                   2005020745
                                   LC

**Published in
the United States**
PMB16A
350 Fifth Ave.
Suite 3308
New York, NY
10118

**Published
in Canada**
616 Welland Ave.,
St. Catharines, Ontario
Canada
L2M 5V6

**Published in the
United Kingdom**
73 Lime Walk
Headington
Oxford
OX3 7AD
United Kingdom

**Published
in Australia**
386 Mt. Alexander Rd.,
Ascot Vale (Melbourne)
VIC 3032

Contents

What are ants?

Ants are **insects**. Insects are **invertebrates**. Invertebrates are animals that do not have **backbones**. Instead of having backbones, insects have hard coverings called **exoskeletons** on the outside of their bodies. Ants are **social insects**. Social insects work together to find food, build homes, and raise their young. Ants live in groups called **colonies**.

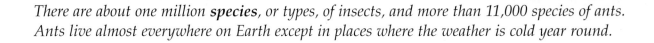

*There are about one million **species**, or types, of insects, and more than 11,000 species of ants. Ants live almost everywhere on Earth except in places where the weather is cold year round.*

worker

male

queen

Three castes of ants

There are three **castes**, or kinds, of ants in a colony: **workers**, **males**, and **queens**. Every colony has many worker ants. Workers are wingless female ants that cannot make babies. They are the smallest ants in the colony— but they do most of the work! Workers collect food, build and clean the **nest**, and take care of the colony's eggs and its young ants. A colony has only a few male ants. Male ants have only one job. They **mate**, or join together with a queen to make babies. A colony usually has only one queen. The queen is a female ant. She is the largest and most important ant in the colony. A queen spends most of her life laying eggs. A baby ant hatches from each egg.

Ant anatomy

Like the bodies of all insects, an ant's body is divided into three main sections. The head makes up one section of an ant's body. An ant has eyes, **antennae**, and **mandibles**, or jaws, on its head. The middle section of an ant's body is called the **thorax**. An ant has six legs attached to its thorax. The third section of an ant's body is called the **abdomen**. An ant has a **petiole**, or narrow waist, between its thorax and its abdomen. The abdomen contains an ant's stomach, heart, and **reproductive parts**. Some ants have stingers on their abdomens.

Thin-winged insects

Ants belong to a group of insects called *Hymenoptera*. This group also includes wasps and bees. The insects in this group have wings that are thin enough to see through. Only queen ants and male ants have wings. A winged ant has two pairs of wings—a large front pair and a small back pair. The wings are attached to the ant's thorax. When the ant flies, the front and back wings on each of its sides hook together and move as a single wing.

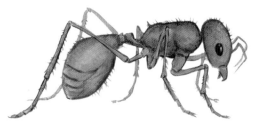

Ant antennae

An ant uses its antennae to smell, to touch, to feel, and to send messages to other ants. An ant can move its antennae forward or backward to investigate its surroundings.

← antennae →

An ant uses its mandibles for cutting, holding, fighting, and digging.

An ant has small mouthparts called **maxillae** for chewing food.

An ant has two **compound eyes**. Compound eyes are made up of many small parts called **eyelets**.

An ant uses its front legs to touch objects and to wash its body.

Lively legs

An ant has **joints** in its legs. A joint is a place where two body parts come together. Your knees and elbows are joints. Joints allow an ant's legs to bend. An ant also has claws at the end of each leg. It uses its claws for grasping.

Ant colonies

An ant colony may contain only a few ants or more than one million ants! Most species of ants live in nests. A nest provides the ants in a colony with shelter and a safe place to raise young ants. Different species of ants live in different types of nests. Some species of ants build their nests under the ground, whereas others build nests above ground.

Nests above the ground

Many ant species that live in warm places build their nests above ground, using leaves, sticks, and soil. Tropical weaver ants, shown left, build their nests in trees. They work as a group to build nests by fastening together leaves. Carpenter ants build nests in tree trunks. They chew through the wood to make nests. Some ant species build nests inside the stems and leaves of plants.

*To fasten together leaves for their nests, weaver ant workers use the **silk** made in the bodies of developing weaver ants. The silk is sticky and acts like a glue that holds the leaves together.*

Underground nests

Many ant species build their nests in the ground. These ants may tunnel as far as 40 feet (12.2 m) into the ground! An underground nest is made up of tunnels and rooms. Each tunnel leads to a different room. Every room has a different use. The queen lays eggs in one room. Other rooms are **nurseries** for young ants. Some rooms are used to store food. Ants even build rooms to hold garbage! Worker ants discard food scraps and other waste in garbage rooms.

These fire ants are among the many ant species that build their nests under the ground.

Home away from home

Army ants travel during the night, searching for food. During the day, they build a **temporary**, or short-term, nest called a **bivouac**. To make a bivouac, army ants join themselves together using their claws and mandibles, as shown right. The ants attach the bivouac to a rock, to a log, or to another surface. The queen ant and young ants are inside the middle of the nest, where they are safe.

What is a life cycle?

Every animal goes through a set of changes called a **life cycle**. First, an animal is born or hatches from an egg. Its body then begins to grow and change until the animal is **mature**, or an adult. Mature animals can make babies. With each baby, a new life cycle begins.

Life span

An animal's life cycle is not the same as its **life span**. A life span is the length of time an animal is alive. The three castes of ants have different life spans. Workers may live only a few weeks or for several years. Most queens live for five years or longer, but the queens of some species can live for up to fifteen years. Male ants live for only a few weeks.

Ants have longer life spans than many other insects have.

From egg to adult

There are four stages in an ant's life cycle: egg, **larva**, **pupa**, and adult. An ant's body changes completely as it goes through its life cycle. This total body change is called **metamorphosis**. An ant begins its life cycle inside an egg. When it hatches, the developing ant is called a larva. The larva eats and grows. It soon becomes a pupa. Its metamorphosis is complete when the pupa has changed into an adult ant. The life cycle of a queen ant is shown below.

egg

larva

pupa

adult queen

Ant eggs

A colony's queen ant lays all the eggs inside the nest. She lays them in a part of the nest called the **egg-laying chamber**. Ant eggs are tiny and smooth. They are white in color and oval in shape. Inside each egg, there is a developing ant called an **embryo**. There is also a **yolk**. The embryo feeds on the yolk.

Tons of tiny eggs

Most ant eggs are about 0.02 inches (0.05 cm) around. Different species of queen ants lay different numbers of eggs. The eggs are small. Hundreds or even thousands of eggs can fit in one egg-laying chamber. Fire ant queens may lay 100 eggs per hour, whereas African driver ant queens may lay thousands of eggs per hour!

Ant nannies

As soon as the queen lays the eggs, worker ants carry the eggs to the **egg chambers**, using their mandibles. An egg chamber is the room where the workers care for the eggs. They care for the eggs by licking the outsides with their tongues. Licking the eggs keeps them free of **bacteria**. Bacteria are tiny living things that cause diseases.

On the move

Worker ants sometimes move the eggs to different egg chambers within the nest. They move them to the warmest egg chambers. Warm temperatures help the embryos grow. During the day, while the sun is shining, the egg chambers near the nest's entrance are the warmest. At night, the egg chambers deep in the nest are the warmest.

Instead of moving the eggs one by one, workers move the eggs in clumps. To make the clumps, the workers lick the eggs. Licking makes the eggs stick together.

Ant larvae

While they are inside eggs, the embryos develop and their bodies grow larger. The eggs begin to swell and turn **transparent**, or clear. The embryos have changed into larvae.

Larvae hatch from the eggs. Once they hatch, the second stage of their life cycles begins.

Always eating!

Ant larvae look like small worms. They have no eyes or legs, but they can bend and move their bodies a little. The larvae are covered with short fine hairs and have tiny heads with mandibles for eating. They are always eating! The young worker ants **regurgitate**, or spit up, food stored inside their bodies. They feed the larvae this food.

Worker ants feed, clean, and care for the larvae. Caring for the larvae is a full-time job! Workers keep the larvae in certain rooms within the nest. They move the larvae to the warmest rooms, just as they moved the eggs.

14

Molting

As larvae grow, their exoskeletons become too tight. The larvae need to **molt**, or shed their exoskeletons. Most larvae molt three times. With each molt, the larvae grow between 0.2 to 1 inches (0.5-2.5 cm). The period of growth between each molt is called an **instar**.

A tight group

The larvae grow more hair each time they molt. The hairs hook the larvae together, allowing the workers to move the larvae from one nursery to another. After their last molts, the groups of larvae are too heavy for the workers to carry. The larvae must now be moved one at a time.

egg

Most queens lay eggs continually. As a result, there are often many ants at different stages of their life cycles within a colony. For example, a larva on the right will soon hatch from its egg. The larvae will then become larger and grow fine hairs on its body, like the other larvae around it.

Growing up

After their last molts, many species of ant larvae spin thin, silky threads in their bodies. The threads come out of their mouths. The larvae wrap the threads around their bodies until they are covered. The silky coverings create sticky **cocoons**. The cocoons are about the size of jellybeans. While the larvae are spinning their cocoons, worker ants cover the larvae with leaves and dirt to protect them. When the larvae finish spinning, the cocoons are uncovered. The workers lick the cocoons to remove any remaining dirt. Inside the cocoons, the larvae become pupae and the third stage of their life cycles begins.

pupa

larva

This worker ant is caring for the white larvae as they prepare to spin their cocoons. The brown cocoons around the larvae contain pupae.

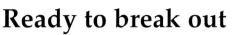

Complete changes

Inside the cocoons, the pupae continue to go through metamorphosis. Their bodies change completely. All pupae grow legs and antennae. Their legs and antennae are folded up against their bodies. Wings grow on the bodies of the male and the queen pupae. Workers do not have to feed the pupae because pupae do not eat.

Ready to break out

After about eight weeks, the pupae have changed into adult ants. Their metamorphosis is complete. The adult ants are ready to break out of their cocoons. They use their mandibles to cut themselves out of the cocoons. Workers may also help the new adult ants cut through their cocoons.

The top of this cocoon has been peeled away to show a pupa's changing body. The pupa's legs and antennae have started to form. Some species of ants do not spin cocoons—their bodies are not covered as they go through metamorphosis.

17

Adult ants

New adult ants are called **callows**. A callow's body is pale, soft, and weak. During the first hours that it is out of the cocoon, the callow's body darkens and its exoskeleton hardens. Most of the new adult ants are workers. The rest of the new ants are males and queens.

Forming a swarm

After they hatch, new worker ants begin their jobs inside their nests. The male and queen ants use their wings to fly out of their nests. All the male and queen ants from nearby colonies also fly out of their nests at the same time. In some ant species, thousands of males and queens form a **swarm**, or a large group of flying ants. All the ants in the swarm mate.

These ants have left their nests and are preparing to join a swarm.

18

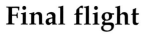

Final flight

When a male ant mates with a queen ant, **sperm** from the male ant's body passes into the body of the queen. The sperm **fertilizes** some of the eggs that are inside the queen's body. Soon after mating, the male ant dies.

The male ant below has finished mating. He will live only a few days.

Two kinds of eggs

Not all ants hatch from the same kinds of eggs. Female ants—workers and queens—hatch from **fertilized eggs**. Fertilized eggs came into contact with sperm inside the queen's body. Male ants hatch from **unfertilized eggs**. Unfertilized eggs did not come into contact with sperm inside the queen's body.

New colonies

After mating, the queens spread out and land on the ground. They tear off their wings. Each queen then starts building her own nest by digging into the soil where she landed. Within hours, the queen has dug the first tunnel of the nest. Once the queen has built her nest, she usually never leaves it.

Forming a colony

Inside the nest, the queen starts laying eggs. She can live for weeks, or even months, without food while she cares for the first eggs she lays. Only workers hatch from these eggs. When the queen lays more eggs, the first group of workers cares for the new eggs. These new eggs will grow to be workers, as well. Over the next few years, the number of workers grows. Eventually, there are enough ants to form a large colony.

While this queen ant is above ground digging her nest, she is in danger of being eaten by other insects and birds.

20

The next generation

After a few years, the new colony has about 10,000 workers. The queen now begins to lay eggs that will hatch into males and new queens. After the males and queens hatch from these eggs, they leave the nest and join a swarm. Eventually, these new queens will build colonies of their own.

This queen ant is laying eggs.

Extra care

The eggs that hatch into males and queens are given extra care. These eggs are kept in their own egg chambers, away from the other eggs. When the larvae hatch from these eggs, a team of workers feeds the larvae often and provides them with extra food and nutrients. The extra food and nutrients help the larvae develop into queens and males. Some scientists believe that these larvae need extra food in order to develop wings and the body parts they will need for mating. Adult males and queens are usually larger than the rest of the ants in the colony are. The worker ants, shown right, are caring for a queen larva.

Worker ants

Most of the ants in a colony are workers. Some worker ants perform jobs inside the nest, whereas others have jobs outside the nest. In some colonies, ants have the same jobs throughout their lives. In other colonies, workers change jobs as they become older.

These leaf-cutter ants work outside the nest. They gather leaves to bring back to the colony. Ants rarely get lost because they use the same routes over and over again.

All work and no play

There is always a lot of activity going on inside an ant nest. Ants take turns sleeping, so work is being done around the clock. Different groups of workers perform different roles in the colony. Some workers build extra rooms in the nest. They may also repair damaged tunnels and rebuild parts of the nest if there is a flood. Forager ants are worker ants that leave the nest to **forage**, or search for food, for the rest of the colony. Midden ants are worker ants that remove garbage and waste from the nest.

Soldiers

Some ant species have a fourth ant caste called **soldiers**. Soldiers guard the entrance to the nest and defend the nest from other ant colonies and animals. Soldiers usually have larger heads than those of the other ants in their colonies. They also have large, powerful mandibles that they use for biting intruders.

This forager ant has caught an insect, which it will bring back to the nest to feed to the other ants.

Ant communication

Ant nests are busy places! Hundreds or even thousands of workers perform different jobs at the same time. Workers must **communicate**, or send messages to one another, in order to make sure that all the work gets done. Ants have **glands** inside their bodies that help them communicate. Each gland produces a different chemical, and each chemical sends a different **signal**, or message, to other ants in the colony. Ants **detect**, or sense, the chemicals with their antennae. They can recognize other ants from the colony by their chemical signals.

Ants also use their antennae to detect intruders. The soldier ant on the left has detected a large red harvester ant, which has wandered too close to the soldier's nest.

24

Leaving a trail

Ants pass chemical signals to one another in different ways. Sometimes they release the chemicals into the air. At other times, they spread the chemicals on the ground. If a worker finds food away from the nest, it turns and walks back to the nest. As it walks, it leaves a chemical trail, which is called a **scent trail**. Other workers in the nest then follow the scent trail back to the food.

Warning!

When an ant senses danger, such as a caterpillar in the nest, it immediately runs around in circles and produces a chemical signal that warns other ants of the danger. Soldier ants rush to attack the intruder. Other ants prepare to move the eggs, larvae, and pupae to safer spots in the nest.

These ants are following a scent trail left by a worker ant from their colony. The scent trail leads the ants to food that the worker has found.

25

An ant's appetite

Many ants are **predators**, or animals that hunt other animals for food. They set out in groups to attack **prey**. Prey are animals eaten by predators. Army ants are predators that travel in large numbers.

As they travel, army ants can eat tens of thousands of animals, including other insects, lizards, snakes, farm animals, and birds. Army ants attack their prey in swarms. They can kill large animals in a few minutes.

Ant dairies

Other species of ants eat plants, seeds, or **fungi**. Some ants are like dairy farmers. They "milk" the liquid produced in the bodies of **aphids**, in the same way that farmers milk cows. Aphids produce a sweet-tasting liquid inside their bodies. Ants stroke the bodies of the aphids to release the liquid. The ants then feed on the liquid. In exchange for food, these ants care for and protect aphids from insect predators, such as ladybugs and lacewings.

Feeding one another

Some ants do not leave the nest, so they are given food by forager ants. When it is hungry, the stay-at-home ant strokes the forager ant's head with its antennae. This action tells the forager ant to regurgitate some food into its mouth. The forager ant then deposits the food from its mouth into the mouth of the other ant.

The green tree forager ant on the left is feeding another ant from the colony.

Ants in danger!

Ants are important animals in their **habitats**. The tunnels and nests they make in soil carry **oxygen** and water to plant roots, helping plants grow. By helping plants grow, ants help many insects and other animals have enough food to eat. When ants eat other insects, they help keep the **populations** of these insects from growing too large. Ants are also food for many other animals, including birds, toads, other insects, and, of course, anteaters!

Under threat

Many ant species live in **rain forests**. Scientists have found as many as 40 different species of ants on a single tree in a rain forest! The biggest threat to ants living in rain forests is **habitat loss**. Habitat loss is the shrinking of the areas in which animals live and find food. People cause habitat loss in rain forests by **clearing**, or removing the trees from, these areas. People clear areas of rain forests to create farmland or to build homes. Thousands of ants are killed when rain forests are cleared. Some ant species live only in rain forests. Scientists are concerned that entire species of ants may be wiped out before we know anything about them.

Helping ants

You can help ants by spreading the word about why they are such amazing creatures! You can also play a role in protecting ant habitats. Talk to your family, friends, and neighbors about taking care of the environment.

Encourage your family to avoid using **pesticides** on the lawn or in the garden. Pesticides are dangerous for ants and many other animals. Taking care of the Earth is good for ants and all other living things.

Keeping ants

Watching an art farm is a great way to study ants up close. You can purchase an ant **terrarium**, or container, at a pet store, or build your own at home. A fish tank with tiny air holes in the lid (like a mesh covering) will provide plenty of space for your ants to build a nest. Fill the tank with damp soil or sand, add some leaves, twigs, and stones. Do not forget to give your ants food, such as crumbs or dead insects, and a small container of water. For step-by-step instructions, visit a how-to website such as www.antcam.com.

Ants online

Do you want to learn more about ants?
Check out these interesting websites:
- http://library.thinkquest.org/C004404/
- www.bubblegum-productions.com/anthony/ants.htm
- www.infowest.com/life/aants.htm

Glossary

Note: Boldfaced words that are defined in the text may not appear in the glossary.

backbone A group of bones in the middle of an animal's back

cocoon A silky case that an insect larva spins around itself before it becomes a pupa

embryo A living thing in the early stage of its life, before it is born or hatches

fertilize To add sperm to an egg so a baby can form

fungi Living things, such as molds and mushrooms, which get their food from both living and dead things

gland A body part that produces and releases a substance

habitat The natural place where an animal lives

nest The home of an ant colony

nursery An area inside ant nests where developing ants are given care

oxygen A gas present in air that humans, animals, and plants need to breathe

pesticide A chemical that kills insects

population The total number of a type of plant or animal living in a certain place

rain forest A forest that receives over 80 inches (203 cm) of rain per year

reproductive parts The body parts an animal uses to make babies

silk A fine strong thread produced inside the bodies of ant larvae

sperm A male reproductive fluid that joins with a female's egg to produce babies

Index

1 2 3 4 5 6 7 8 9 0 Printed in the U.S.A. 4 3 2 1 0 9 8 7 6 5